Planets

A LEGO® ADVENTURE IN THE REAL WORLD

By Penelope Arlon and
Tory Gordon-Harris

> 3, 2, 1 . . . BLASTOFF! Let's zoom into space and discover new worlds!

SCHOLASTIC

New York Toronto London Auckland
Sydney Mexico City New Delhi Hong Kong

Welcome, LEGO fans!

LEGO® Minifigures show you the world in a unique nonfiction program.

This book is part of a program of LEGO® nonfiction books, with something for all the family, at every age and stage. LEGO nonfiction books have amazing facts, beautiful real-world photos, and minifigures everywhere, leading the fun and discovery.

To find out about the books in the program, visit www.scholastic.com.

ISBN 978-0-545-94765-7

10 9 8 7 6 5 4 3 2 1   16 17 18 19 20

Printed in the U.S.A.   40
First edition, July 2016

There's so much to explore in space. Come and find me!

Contents

Build it!
There are plenty of ideas for builds that are out of this world as you zoom through this book!

Play it!
Look out for these great ideas for minifigure action. Create space adventures of your own!

I can't wait for you to join me. I could use some company!

I can't wait for my first space adventure to Mars!

3

Let's explore!

Space is the biggest, most incredible thing you can imagine. We find out new facts about stars, planets, and space objects every day.

Hooray! It's taken me ten years to become an astronaut. Time to rocket to the stars!

Slow down! Being an astronaut is more than just flying rockets. You need to learn all about space. Come on, I'll show you . . .

I feel the need for speed, and crazy space machines are superfast! Let's go!

Planet spotting

For thousands of years, people spotted planets in the night sky. Now incredible machines help us see into deep space—and some even travel there!

Mercury, Venus, Mars, Jupiter, and Saturn can be spotted from your own backyard. Just lie down and look up!

Stare hard enough, and you may spot me out there!

Space telescopes can see billions of miles away. But we still want to see farther . . .

Telescopes
The seven closest planets to Earth can all be seen using a home telescope.

Giant telescopes
All over the world, huge telescopes spot faraway planets in distant space.

Space telescopes
Telescopes can see better when they are away from Eart so we send them into space!

Rockets

Everything that travels to space has to be blasted off Earth in rockets. That includes machines and people.

Build it!
Build a space probe that can discover new worlds. Here are some famous space probes.

Galileo

Magellan

Stardust

Rosetta

Juno

LADEE

> Space probes do not have people on them. Send ME out to explore!

> Woo-hoo! We're off!

Build it bigger!
Probes have huge panels, like wings, that unfold to catch the sunlight. Build two on your space probe.

ace probes
ese small machines travel ough space, sending back ormation and photos.

Humans
We've been to the Moon, and soon we'll be visiting Mars, too!

The Sun

The Sun, which lights and heats our planet, is our very own star. It's a superhot ball of fiery gas and is REALLY, REALLY big.

SOLAR PROBE PLUS

Starting in 2018, this space probe will fly around the Sun 24 times, sending red-hot info back to Earth.

Superstar

About 1 million Earths could fit inside the Sun! The Sun's center is 27 million°F (15 million°C). It's so hot that space probes (and spaceships) melt if they get too close.

> Scientists have recorded strange tunes coming out of the Sun. Want to hear some hot rock?

> Gulp! Can't we hear it on a radio?

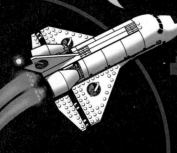

HOT FACT

A piece of the Sun's center the size of a pinhead would be so hot it would be deadly to people 100 miles (161 km) away!

MEDIUM STAR

Our Sun is only a
medium-size star.
There are some
stars in space
that are 100
times bigger!

Ah! The Sun is
a real star, just like me.
There aren't very many REAL
stars out there.

Actually, there
are about 1 billion
trillion other stars
out there . . .

Our solar system

Our Sun is at the center of a family of planets and rocks called the solar system. Eight planets and millions of rocks all move around the Sun in circles, called orbits.

Mercury
Venus
Earth
Mars

Rocky planets
The first four planets, nearest the Sun, are made of rock. They are the smallest planets.

Gas giants
The four planets farthest from the Sun are made of gas. The gas planets are COLOSSAL!

JUPITER
Jupiter is the largest of all our Sun's planets.

Everything moves around the Sun because of GRAVITY. The Sun is a bit like a magnet, pulling everything toward it. Nothing floats away. That's gravity.

Space rocks

In between Mars and Jupiter are billions of rocks. These rocks are known as the asteroid belt. They travel around the Sun, too. Beyond Neptune are more icy rocks, and maybe even a giant ninth planet, called Planet X.

NEPTUNE

Neptune is the farthest planet from the Sun.

SATURN

Huge rocky rings surround Saturn.

URANUS

Uranus is very cold and very dark.

Mercury

If you travel outward from the Sun, the first planet you get to is the smallest and speediest, Mercury. It is superhot! Hotter than your oven at full heat. Ouch!

Mercury

MESSENGER

The NASA space probe *MESSENGER* took six and a half years to reach Mercury. It was tricky to catch up with it because the planet moves so fast! In 2011, *MESSENGER* took the first good pictures of Mercury.

An atmosphere is a thick layer of gases that surrounds some planets, including ours. It protects the planet, like a blanket. Mercury has no atmosphere.

SUN POWER

Solar panels on the probe made electricity from sunlight. They powered the probe through space.

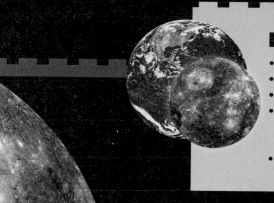

PLANET STATS

- Made of: Rock and metal
- Moons: 0
- Rings: 0
- Distance from Sun: 40 million miles (58 million km)
- Space probe missions: 2

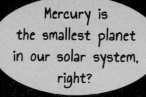

BAM SLAM

With no atmosphere, Mercury gets smashed by space rocks!

> Mercury is the smallest planet in our solar system, right?

Smash!

Mercury's ground is full of holes, called craters, because of the space rocks that slam into it. It's a dangerous place to be!

> Yes! And it's set to hold that record. Mercury is shrinking! Just like this hot dog! Yum!

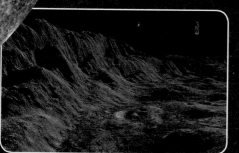

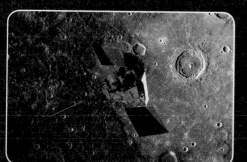

Crash!

In 2015, *MESSENGER* flew down to the surface of Mercury. It sent back information as it crashed into the planet and left a crater 50 feet (15 m) wide!

Venus

The second planet from the Sun is Venus. Venus is like Earth's evil twin. It is nearly the same size as Earth and has clouds and weather like Earth does. But unlike Earth, it is very, very poisonous and very, very hot.

Phew, stinky!

Venus has a thick atmosphere, which means that it has weather, like Earth does. But it is ALWAYS cloudy on Venus. Scientists think that the air might smell like rotten eggs—yuck!

MAGELLAN

In the 1990s, the space probe *Magellan* flew near Venus and mapped it for us.

> Venus is named after the Roman god of love.

> Venus sounded romantic, but this is no honeymoon resort.

> They say it's hot enough to melt plas outside, and the air superpoisonous.

Steamy hot

When the Sun's heat hits Venus, the clouds trap it in. So it gets hotter and hotter. Even hotter than Mercury!

PLANET STATS

- Made of: Rock and metal
- Moons: 0
- Rings: 0
- Distance from Sun:
  67 million miles
  (108 million km)
- Space probe missions: 41

MAAT MONS

The highest volcano on Venus is known as Maat Mons. The crater is ENORMOUS!

Ha! Those Earthlings don't seem to be able to survive anywhere.

Let's head for the Moon, Honey!

15

Earth

Our own planet, Earth, is the third planet from the Sun. It is covered in water and is the only planet known to have life. That makes it really special.

Water

Water is the reason why plants and animals can live on Earth. If we can find another planet or moon with water on it, there might be life there, too.

We have better maps of Mars than of our own ocean floor.

Hmm, that's not very helpful . . .

PLANET STATS

- Made of: Rock and metal
- 70% of surface covered in water
- Moons: 1
  - Rings: 0
    - Distance from Sun:
      93 million miles
      (150 million km)
      - Space probe missions:
        Exploration happening
        all the time

Atmosphere

Our planet is surrounded
by a thick atmosphere
that protects it from
flying rocks. It also
gives us clouds
and weather.

Do you think
that aliens look
like people?

Well, look at the
difference between lions and
butterflies. That shows how
different from us aliens
could be!

ER60082

The Moon

Our Moon is a huge ball of rock that moves around Earth and with us through space. Our Moon is our closest neighbor—but it is still 250,000 miles (402,000 km) from Earth!

MOON SEAS

The dark patches on the Moon are called seas. But they don't have any water in them.

CRATERS

These holes, called craters, show where huge rocks have bashed into the Moon.

What is a moon?

A moon is an object that orbits a planet, held by the planet's gravity. Earth has only one moon, but some other planets have many, many more.

Yawn! Is the Moon made of cheese?

No. The surface of the Moon is rock, covered in a layer of thin dust. Nobody knows what is below the surface, since nobody has dug a big hole yet.

So the inside could be made of cheese?

Moon shapes

The Sun shines only on one side of the Moon. We see different amounts of the lit part as the Moon orbits Earth. That's why the Moon appears to change shape in the sky.

It would take 133 days to drive nonstop to the Moon. Without a snack break? Seriously?

Step on it!

There is no wind on the Moon, so if you make a footprint on it, it will stay forever. This 40-year-old footprint is still there.

Man on the Moon

In 1969, Neil Armstrong was the first man to walk on the Moon. He and another astronaut dropped from their spaceship in a little lander called *Eagle*.

Sigh . . . very unlikely.

DRIVING ON THE MOON

In 1972, astronaut Eugene Cernan drove 21 miles (34 km) on the Moon. This photograph shows Cernan checking over the lunar rover, before loading up and heading out.

PLAY IT!
Take your astronauts to the Moon and help them explore. What will they find?

Only 12 people have ever walked on the Moon. In 1972, Eugene Cernan left Earth on the Apollo 17 mission. He traveled to the Moon and was the last person to walk on it. Nobody has been there since. The exciting thing about the trip was that he brought a car with him. He got to drive around in the lunar rover! It couldn't go very fast, because it's pretty rocky on the Moon. But it still holds the record for the fastest-moving land vehicle away from Earth!

Just before heading back to Earth, Cernan wrote his daughter Tracy's initials, TDC, in the dust. They will be there forever . . . or until the next Moon visitor rubs them out!

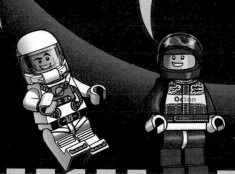

Did you know that the lunar rover goes only 8 miles per hour (13 kph)?

Are you kidding me? All that space to race, and I could RUN faster than that!

A baseball pitch would travel faster on the Moon than Earth, as there is no atmosphere to slow it down.

Far out, man . . .

Play it! Here are some ideas . . .

 1 *Do your astronauts have a vehicle?*

 2 *Are there any other visitors to the Moon?*

 3 *Is the Moon made of cheese? Or maybe gold?*

Stargazing

Look into the sky on a clear night—it's full of stars. Thousands of years ago, people joined the stars into shapes that they could recognize, like making connect-the-dots drawings. The shapes are called constellations. Learn how to spot some.

I'm the dazzling queen of the stars.

You'll impress everyone if you can point this one out!

Anyone seen my bone?

The Big Dipper
This shape is one of the easiest to spot in the night sky.

Cassiopeia (queen)
This constellation was named after Cassiopeia, a Greek queen.

Canis Major (dog)
Sirius, the brightest star in the sky is part of this group of stars.

The Milky Way

All the stars that we can see are in our galaxy, the Milky Way. A galaxy is a vast family of stars that move together. Our Sun is one of billions of stars in the Milky Way.

Rooooarrrr!

The sky is not the place for fish . . .

Me see bull in sky . . .

Pisces (fish)
The fish constellation is huge but quite faint.

Taurus (bull)
10,000-year old cave paintings show the bull.

Draco (dragon)
This dragon wraps itself around the North Star.

Mars

Mars is red. It looks red hot, but it is actually freezing cold because it is farther away from the Sun than Earth is. Despite this, astronauts are still racing to get there!

Mars takeover
Mars is the easiest planet for us to send people to. We have already sent robot rovers, like Curiosity, to sniff around for us.

PLANET STATS

- Made of: Rock and metal
- Moons: 2
- Rings: 0
- Distance from Sun: 142 million miles (229 million km)
- Space probe missions: 44

MINI MOONS
Mars has two tiny moons. Phobos is much smaller than our Moon, and Deimos is even smaller than Phobos.

Hey, I'm here, you know.

Sigh . . . I'm bored. I can't wait for those Earthlings to get here . . .

Wanted: people willing to go to Mars. Here are a few things that you need to know …

I'll need some great music!

It's going to be at least a three-year trip.

Okay! Where's the menu?

No fussy eaters. Food is brought from Earth.

I should have gotten a haircut . . .

There are HUGE dust storms.

Sigh . . . I think I can see America.

Earth is far, far away.

We drink our leftovers.

ALL water is recycled.

No return ticket? Now you tell me, dude!

No one is sure how to get back to Earth.

If you think I'm going to Mars after all that, you must be on another planet!

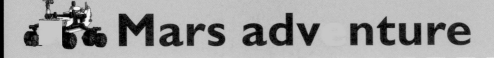

CURIOSITY TAKES SOME AMAZING SELFIES

The Mars rover has a long camera arm that stretches out so that it can photograph itself. It then transmits the photos home to Earth.

PLAY IT!
Take your rover and astronauts to Mars! It's a whole new world of adventure. What will they find on the Red Planet? Will they be safe?

Meet the Curiosity rover. In 2011, this robot vehicle was rocketed off to Mars. Since 2012, it has been on its own Mars adventure. It snoops around, taking photos and sending information back all the time. Curiosity has not bumped into any Martians yet, but it is always looking for signs of life.

So far, Curiosity has made some useful discoveries. It has drilled down into the rock and found that there might have been life on Mars millions of years ago. It has tested the air to see if it would be safe for humans to visit. Scientists now think that there is water on Mars. Will Curiosity explore it? And even find living creatures? We can't wait to find out!

I'd better get MY skates on . . . !

Curiosity is woken up every Mars day with a song from Earth!

Breaking news! Water on Mars, 30 miles (48 km) from Curiosity. Go check it out!

Umm, Curiosity travels only 6 feet (2 m) a minute!

Play it! Here are some ideas . . .

1 Do your astronauts have a rover to ride on?

2 If you dig under the surface, what will you find?

3 Do aliens live on Mars?

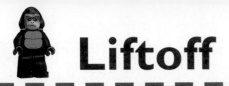

Liftoff

It takes a lot of power to blast a spacecraft into space. The spacecraft is attached to a huge rocket that has to be superpowerful to get itself off the ground.

Soyuz

The *Soyuz* rocket can take three astronauts into space. It takes off from Kazakhstan, in Asia. There are four stages of liftoff.

STAGE THREE

About five minutes after takeoff, a large section of the rocket falls off. The rocket is now 105 miles (169 km) high.

STAGE TWO

After about two minutes, the rocket drops the four boosters to the ground. It is about 25 miles (40 km) up in the sky.

STAGE ONE

Liftoff! The four boosters blast the rocket into the air.

SUPER SPEED

The rocket travels at 25,000 miles per hour (40,200 kph)!

STAGE FOUR

After nine minutes, the last engine is dropped and the spacecraft is free. It is about 140 miles (225 km) high, and in space.

ASTRONAUTS

The astronauts are in a small capsule inside this section. They can't see out until stage four.

He also said that suddenly going into zero gravity is like being thrown off a cliff. Gulp!

Oooof, yes, that's exactly what it feels like.

3, 2, 1 . . . whoooaaa! The Canadian astronaut Chris Hadfield flew three space missions. He said that takeoff feels like having a big gorilla sitting on you.

Blastoff!

Check out these strange things that have been blasted off Earth and carried into space!

Fruit flies

Let's go!

3, 2, 1 . .

Blastoff!

MINIFIGURES

Three special LEGO® minifigures are traveling to Jupiter right now!

SANDWICH

A hungry astronaut once smuggled up a corned beef sandwich!

LIGHTSABER

Luke Skywalker's lightsaber from the *Star Wars* movies flew into space.

In 1960, Strelka the dog flew into space. She later had six puppies. One of the pups was given to the president of the United States.

White mouse

MOON TREES

In 1971, 500 tree seeds were taken to the Moon and back. They were all planted on Earth and are known as "Moon trees."

"Jingle Bells" on a harmonica was the first song to be played in space.

SPACE TOURIST

Richard Garriott paid $30 million to spend ten days on the ISS.

DINOSAUR

A Coelophysis skull traveled on the space shuttle *Endeavour*.

CHIMPANZEE

Ham the chimp was sent into space and returned safely.

The ISS astronauts played soccer in space to celebrate the 2014 World Cup. Hey! Where'd the ball go?

TORCH

The Olympic torch went into space, but it was too dangerous to light it!

Space walk adventure

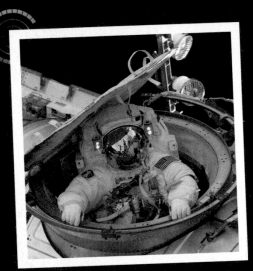

ASTRONAUTS BUILDING THE ISS

These photographs show brave astronauts space walking. They are building and mending the ISS ... while wearing huge gloves!

PLAY IT!
Now build your own astronauts and send them on space walk adventures!

Building a lab in outer space

The International Space Station (ISS) is an enormous science lab, as big as a soccer field. It orbits Earth about 200 miles (322 km) up in space, moving at about 17,500 miles per hour (28,200 kph). But how did it get up there?

Building it was a real space adventure! It was rocketed up in thousands of pieces. Then astronauts had to build it. Building began in 1998, and astronauts are still adding and mending parts. The astronauts have to put on huge space suits, then climb out of the space station to work on it. They are attached by ropes so they don't float away. They have to be expert builders as well as astronauts!

> Okay, put on those gloves and get out there . . . We need a new toilet.

> But I can barely hold this wrench! These gloves are ENORMOUS!

> The longest space walk was 8 hours and 56 minutes, so we'd better get going. I think I need the bathroom!

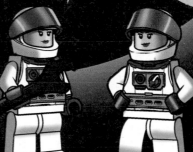

Play it! Now invent your own . . .

 1 *What are your astronauts building in space?*

 2 *Is there any chance they will float away?*

 3 *What can they see from space?*

The space suit

The space suits that astronauts wear on space walks are like mini spaceships. Everything that an astronaut needs to live is built into the suit—even the toilet!

Hot or cold?
It is really, really cold in space. But if the Sun is shining on you, it's burning hot. Space suits protect from the cold and the heat.

GLOVES

Gloves have heated fingertips to keep hands warm.

DIAPER

Astronauts wear superthick underwear so that they don't have to return to the space station to go to the bathroom!

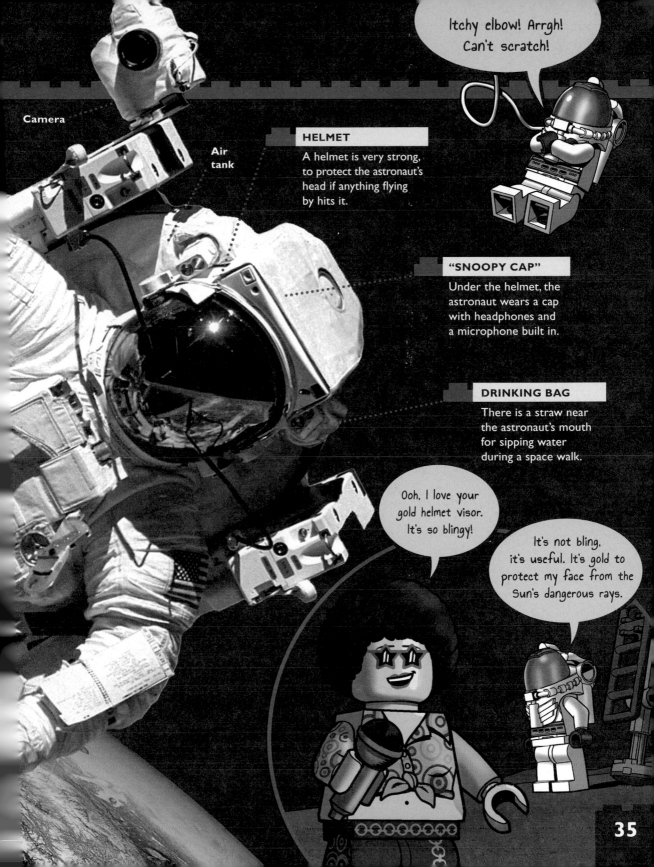

Itchy elbow! Arrgh! Can't scratch!

Camera

Air tank

HELMET
A helmet is very strong, to protect the astronaut's head if anything flying by hits it.

"SNOOPY CAP"
Under the helmet, the astronaut wears a cap with headphones and a microphone built in.

DRINKING BAG
There is a straw near the astronaut's mouth for sipping water during a space walk.

Ooh, I love your gold helmet visor. It's so blingy!

It's not bling, it's useful. It's gold to protect my face from the Sun's dangerous rays.

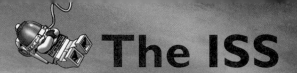

The ISS

A crew of six astronauts live on the International Space Station (ISS) at one time. Each stays for about six months. Life is very strange on the ISS.

She has even wilder hair than I do!

Delivery!
All the food has to be delivered to the ISS by spacecraft. The *Progress* spacecraft flies without anyone on it and locks onto the ISS.

Zero gravity
There is no gravity on the ISS, so food floats away and hair stands on end. Even water floats away in bubbles!

Sleep well!
Astronauts have to strap themselves to the walls when they sleep. Otherwise, they float around and bump into things.

A cheese and salami pizza was once delivered to the ISS. It traveled at over 16,000 miles per hour (25,700 kph). Now that's fast food!

Build it!
Your astronauts need a space base. Design a space station. Here are some of the important parts.

Solar panels

Living quarters

Docking station

Viewing window

Laboratory

Radiator

GIANT TRASH CAN
The astronauts send the *Progress* spacecraft away with all their garbage!

Space lettuce
Astronauts are trying to grow food in space. They recently grew some salad greens. It was the first food grown away from Earth!

Build it bigger!
Now that you've made your space station, build a delivery probe that can attach to it. Something needs to take out the trash!

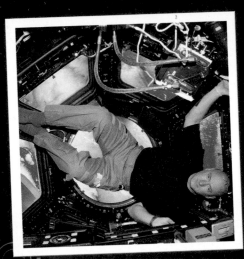

SCOTT KELLY ON THE ISS

Floating fruit nearly drove Scott Kelly bananas on the ISS. But at least the views of Earth were great from the space station.

> PLAY IT!
> What adventures will your astronauts have on your ISS?

The next big step in space travel is to rocket a person to Mars. But will that make human bones turn to jelly? Or brains go squishy? It's time to test a human. In March 2015, astronaut Scott Kelly was one of two space travelers blasted off Earth to spend a whole year on the ISS. No other American has spent as much time in space as Scott has! His body was tested from top to bottom.

During that year, Scott exercised for over 700 hours. He drank 193 gallons (730 L) of recycled urine and sweat . . . yuck! He also did about 383 tests on his body. Scott has an identical twin brother here on Earth who was tested, too, to compare how their bodies behaved. Mars, here we come!

So if we drink our pee and sweat, what happens to astronaut poop?

Well, actually, it burns up in our atmosphere and looks like shooting stars.

Are you telling me that the next time I make a wish on a shooting star, I'll be wishing on astronaut poop?

Play it! Here are some ideas . . .

 Do they feel strange floating around?

 Will they spot other spaceships?

 What happens if an alien arrives?

The asteroid belt

Asteroids are rocks that orbit the Sun. There are millions of asteroids that float around between Mars and Jupiter. This ring of rocks is known as the asteroid belt.

KLEOPATRA

The asteroid Kleopatra looks like a dog's bone!

Ragged rocks

Asteroids can be 20 feet (6 m) to 500 miles (805 km) across! They come in lots of different shapes. None of them is completely round.

Most people think that the dinosaurs were wiped out because a big space rock hit Earth.

That's not such a bad thing . . . Arrgh!

Gold rush! I've heard that there's an asteroid filled with gold. People are already racing to mine it. It's mine!

HAYABUSA
The space probe is about the size of a car.

Touchdown
The Japanese space probe *Hayabusa* left Earth in 2003 to visit the asteroid Itokawa. It took samples of the soil and brought them back to Earth in 2010.

Most asteroids that race toward the Earth are burned up into tiny pieces in our atmosphere. The ones that get through are called meteorites.

41

Jupiter

Jupiter is the king of the planets in our solar system. It's so big that all the other planets could fit inside it!

LIGHTNING

Superbolts of lightning on Jupiter are much more powerful than most flashes on Earth.

Gas giant

Jupiter is the gas planet nearest to the Sun. It is a giant ball of gas and liquid. If you flew to Jupiter, there would be no place to land!

Juno

The space probe *Juno* is on its way to Jupiter. It's going to take a peek through the thick clouds for the first time.

Jupiter is the biggest planet, the fastest-spinning planet, and the planet with the biggest moon. It's a record breaker. I know how it feels!

Jupiter's moons

Jupiter has 67 moons (spotted so far!). And 4 of the rocky moons are huge! Io is covered in volcanoes and is constantly spewing sulfur into space.

PLANET STATS

- Made of: Gas
- Moons: 67
- Rings: 3
- Distance from Sun: 484 million miles (779 million km)
- Space probe missions: 9

The weather on Jupiter is windy and wild, and storms can last for hundreds of years. Let's fly by.

What will Juno find? A humongous hurricane? A flaming fireball? Daggerlike ice rain?

Do you mind?

We're playing Snap.

Saturn

Saturn would float in water if there was a bathtub big enough!

Saturn is not as big as Jupiter, but it's still an ENORMOUS ball of gas. It is the most spectacular planet because of the amazing rings around it.

The rings

Saturn has seven rings. Each one is made of billions of pieces of ice. Some pieces are the size of sand grains; others are the size of buses.

Sigh. So beautiful . . .

Not me!

Saturn's sky

The space probe *Cassini* has been poking around Saturn's moons. There are some pretty strange ones.

Mimas

Mimas has a huge crater on it that makes it look like an eyeball!

Tethys

Tethys looks like someone has scribbled across it with red crayon.

PLANET STATS

- Made of: Gas
- Moons: 62
  - Rings: 7
  - Distance from Sun: 886 million miles (1.4 billion km)
- Space probe missions: 4

GIANT DISKS

The rings are only about half a mile (0.8 km) thick—but 24,000 miles (38,600 km) wide!

Half and half!

Brr! Does this melt?

Come and visit soon!

Iapetus

One side is completely black, and the other side is bright white.

Enceladus

Enceladus is a huge ocean covered in a layer of ice.

Titan

Titan is very similar to Earth. Could it have life on it?

PLANET STATS

- Made of: Gas and liquid, with rock in the center
- Moons: 27
- Rings: 13
- Distance from Sun: 1.8 billion miles (2.9 billion km)
- Space probe missions: 1

Uranus and Neptune are far, far away. They are very dark, very cold, and superstormy.

Blue twins

Uranus and Neptune are both swirling balls of gas with rocky centers. Methane gas makes them look blue. Uranus is the only planet that spins tilted, on its side.

URANUS

Uranus has rocky rings around it—but they are not as impressive as Saturn's.

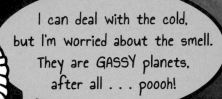

I can deal with the cold, but I'm worried about the smell. They are GASSY planets, after all . . . poooh!

Neptune

PLANET STATS

- Made of: Gas and liquid, with rock in the center
- Moons: 14
- Rings: 6
- Distance from Sun: 2.8 billion miles (4.5 billion km)
- Space probe missions: 1

NEPTUNE

Neptune has the most violent weather in the solar system. Its storms are ten times stronger than hurricanes on Earth.

Voyager 2

In 1977, *Voyager 2* flew into space. It stopped off at Uranus and Neptune to have a look around.

VOYAGER 2

It took the space probe 12 years to reach Neptune!

Voyager 1

In 1977, the *Voyager 1* space probe was launched. Like its twin, *Voyager 2*, it was sent to explore nearby planets, but *Voyager 1* went far beyond. It is now at the edge of the solar system.

FAR, FAR AWAY

Voyager 1 is now over 12 billion miles (19 billion km) away. It's the man-made object the farthest away from Earth.

The aliens will love the Golden Record, especially the music.

I'm sure they'll love all that Bach and Beethoven.

What? No disco?

1980 – Flies by Saturn, 886 million miles (1.4 billion km) away

1977 – Launches from Earth

1979 – Flies by Jupiter, 484 million miles (779 million km) away

2015 – Reaches the edge of the solar system, 12 billion miles (19 billion km) away

The Golden Record

The probe is carrying a golden disc holding photographs, music, animal sounds, and messages from Earth. It is so that aliens can find out what life on Earth is like.

Scientists think there might be a giant planet, Planet X, at the edge of our Solar System. Perhaps Voyager I will spot it.

ANTENNA

The antenna lets Voyager I talk to Earth.

SPEEDY

The probe travels 870,000 miles (1,400,000 km) a day.

INSTRUMENTS

Voyager I is covered in very clever instruments that measure things like temperature. It's pretty chilly out there!

Dwarf Pluto

Pluto's moon Charon

Travel beyond Neptune, and you'll reach a ring called the Kuiper Belt. There are millions of icy objects here. Some of these are round. They are known as dwarf planets.

Planet no more

Pluto was once one of the main planets. Then, in 2006, scientists changed their minds and called it a dwarf planet instead. Poor Pluto.

Headline news! Some scientists think that Pluto should be turned BACK into a main planet again. Make up your minds!

The *New Horizons* probe travels 1 million miles (1.6 million km) a day.

PLUTO

New pictures show that Pluto is covered with mountain ranges, deep valleys, and red and orange patches!

New Horizons

In 2015, the space probe *New Horizons* sent back the first close-up images of Pluto. No aliens have been spotted . . . yet!

ARRGH! A monster with two eyes!

ARRGH! A monster with one eye!

Comet adventure

ROSETTA'S LANDER ON THE COMET

After setting down on the comet, the lander quickly started working. Then it went quiet. Several months later it sprang back into life and sent more data.

PLAY IT!
Send your rock star astronauts out to find and follow a comet! Comets are superspeedy, so it will be tricky to catch one!

Chasing rocking rocks!

A comet is a chunk of icy rock that often starts off in the Kuiper Belt. Then it suddenly gets a push from another rock and is hurled toward the Sun. Comets leave icy tails behind them. They can sometimes be seen shooting across the sky from Earth.

In 2004, a space probe called *Rosetta* was sent out to chase a comet and land on it. After an epic ten-year journey, *Rosetta* reached a comet. It sent a small lander down onto the comet. The comet was traveling at 34,000 miles per hour (55,000 kph), so it was a tricky move!

Rosetta discovered that the 2-mile-wide (3.2 km) comet is so light that it would float on water. It also sniffed the comet and found that it smells of rotten eggs, horse stables, and marzipan. PHEW!

When I asked you if you wanted to see some epic rock, I meant comet watching . . .

No worries. Comets are cool. I hear that they may have metal in them, too . . .

Rock AND heavy metal! Awesome!

Play it! Here are some ideas . . .

1 What will your astronauts travel in?

2 What will they be singing as they arrive?

3 What is the comet made of? Heavy metal?

Exoplanets

In 5 billion years' time, the Sun will begin to die.
NO Sun = NO life! Don't panic. Astronomers
have discovered many other stars in our galaxy
that also have planets. These planets are known
as exoplanets. Time to move!

Kepler space telescope

Kepler, a huge telescope, stares
at the same patch of sky all the
time. It has spotted over 1,000
exoplanets so far.

Kepler

There could be 160 billion
exoplanets out there in the
Milky Way. We've got some
serious house hunting to do!

I can't wait to
see our new home! Are
we there yet?
Are we there yet?

Home away from home

Gliese 832 c has a similar temperature to Earth's, though its sun is not as bright as ours. It could also have water on it. BUT, big problem—it would take us 400,000 years to get to it!

GLIESE 832 C

Kepler is always looking for Earth's twin planet. Gliese 832 c is the planet most similar to Earth that has been found so far.

Do you think we'll find water or flowers or houses, or chocolate?

Nope, looks like we're all alone. Except for that big grey guy . . . !

New home

Could someone rename these planets to something a bit more catchy . . . like Dave or Marge?

There are lots of mega-strange exoplanets that no one would ever want to live on!

OGLE-2005-BLG-390L b
You'll need your skates to get around on this icy planet. It's the coldest planet ever found. Brrrr.

55 Cancri e
This planet is thought to be made of diamonds. And it's eight times the mass of Earth. Bling it on!

Wow, there are some crazy worlds out there!

WASP-12 b

This superhot exoplanet orbits its star so closely that the star is eating it. It has only 10 million years left before it's swallowed whole!

GJ 1214 b

This planet might be nothing but a hot, giant ocean. That's one huge, scorching hot tub!

TrES-2 b

This planet has no light at all. It is seriously dark. Nobody knows why. It just is.

PSO J318.5-22

This planet has no sun! It just drifts around in space with nowhere to go. No sunrises or sunsets—that's too sad.

Far, far away

What will we spot next? The Hubble Space Telescope has already discovered some amazing things. The brand-new James Webb Space Telescope, launching in 2018, is much more powerful than Hubble!

Hubble Space Telescope

Hubble is a telescope that orbits Earth. It has photographed galaxies. It has even spotted two crashing into each other.

Hubble Space Telescope

Galaxies crashing

The star closest to our Sun, Proxima Centauri, is 24,800,000,000,000 miles (39,900,000,000,000 km) away.

Hmm, I could do with my nearest neighbor being that far away . . .

Morning, Bob. Can I read your paper when you finish?

Black holes

Hubble has detected strange things in space called black holes. A black hole is a star that is dying and sucking everything around it into a hole, like water down a drain. It even sucks up light!

If you were sucked into a black hole, your body would stretch. You'd look like this pretzel!

beep erp zig zama

z*rp zepo

Alien life

Are we alone in space? Nobody knows, but scientists are doing their best to find out if there is more life out there. What would an alien look like, if we met one?

WATER BEARS

These tiny Earth creatures can live in space—with no space suits! Perhaps aliens look like this!

What's next?

The study of planets has only just begun. There will be so many more discoveries in the future. Watch this space!

Hotel Moon
Don't book your vacation for 2025 yet. You may be able to visit a Moon hotel!

First on Mars
Jump on the *Orion* spacecraft, and you may be the first to step on Mars!

MISSION: ASTEROID
Next stop—send humans to an asteroid. Then capture it and drag it back to Earth!

My perfect summer job. I get to cook food, serve it, and chase it! I'm over the Moon!

Our future in space

Vacations in space

Sleep travel

Humans on Mars

Space elevator to ISS

Lassoing asteroids

Skintight space suits

Superpowerful James Webb Space Telescope

Glossary

asteroid
A small rocky object that travels around the Sun.

atmosphere
The blanket of gasses that surrounds a planet.

black hole
A dying star that has such strong gravity that it even pulls light into it.

comet
A small, icy object that travels towards and away from the Sun. It does not move in a perfect circle around it.

constellation
A group of stars that form a pattern that can be recognized.

crater
A hole in the ground of a planet caused by a large rock crashing into it.

dwarf planet
A small planet that travels with other groups of rocks around the Sun.

exoplanet
A planet that orbits another star outside our solar system.

galaxy
A group of billions of stars that are held together by gravity and move together in space.

gravity
A force that pulls objects towards it, a bit like a magnet. Earth's gravity stops us from floating away.

lander
A spacecraft that can land on the surface of a space object such as a planet, moon, or comet.

moon
An object that moves around, or orbits, a planet.

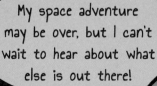

My space adventure may be over, but I can't wait to hear about what else is out there!

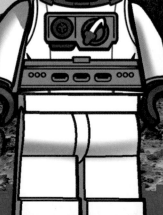

> Come and find us Earthlings! We're out here waiting!

orbit
The journey that a space object takes when it moves around another object in space.

planet
A round object that moves around a star.

rover
A moving vehicle that explores a planet or other object in space.

solar system
A star and everything that travels around it, such as planets and rocks.

space probe
A vehicle that is sent into space to explore and send back information to Earth.

sun
The star that our Earth travels around. It gives us warmth and light.

visor
Part of a space helmet that can be moved down to cover the face.

Build it!
Build an incredible space station for a faraway planet. What will your minifigures need to survive?

Houses

Restaurant

Supermarket

Theater

Swimming pool

Laboratory

Build it bigger!
Now build a giant alien space station! What strange buildings might the aliens have?

Index

Credits

For the LEGO Group: Randi Kirsten Sørensen Assistant Manager; Peter Moorby Licensing Coordinator; Heidi K. Jensen Licensing Manager; Paul Hansford Creative Publishing Manager; Martin Leighton Lindhardt Publishing Graphic Designer

Photographs © cover space background: ESA and A. Nota (STScI/ESA)/NASA; cover center top planet: NASA; cover bottom left planet: NASA; cover bottom right planet: PHL @ UPR Arecibo (phl.upr.edu), ESA/Hubble/NASA; cover top left: JPL/Space Science Institute/NASA; back cover bottom left: Andrey Armyagov/Shutterstock, Inc.; back cover bottom right: NASA; back cover top left: NASA; 1 background: NASA; 2 background: ESA/NASA; 2 center right: JPL-Caltech/NASA; 4-5 space background and throughout: NASA; 4-5 center: Ken Thornsley/NASA; 6 center left Earth: pkproject/Shutterstock, Inc.; 6 bottom left: ClaudioVentrella/iStockphoto; 6 bottom center: WorkinghamOwl/iStockphoto; 6 bottom right background: ESA/Hubble/D. A. Gouliermis/NASA; 6 bottom right Hubble Space Telescope: NASA; 6-7 top rocket: 3DSculptor/iStockphoto; 7 all other images: NASA; 7 right bottom left: JPL/NASA; 7 right bottom right: Ames Research Center/NASA; 8 center right: NASA; 8-9 background: SDO/NASA; 10 sun and planet: Detlev van Ravenswaay/Science Source; 11 top center: Detlev van Ravenswaay/Science Source; 11 center planets: Detlev van

Ravenswaay/Science Source; 12 bottom left: Johns Hopkins University Applied Physics Laboratory/Carnegie Institution of Washington/NASA; 12-13 Mercury: Johns Hopkins University/APL/NASA; 13 top left Earth and throughout: pkproject/Shutterstock, Inc.; 13 bottom left top: Michael Carroll/Alien Volcanoes by Lopes and Carroll, The Johns Hopkins University Press, 2008/NASA; 13 bottom left bottom: Johns Hopkins University Applied Physics Laboratory/Carnegie Institution of Washington/NASA; 13 center asteroid: JPL-Caltech/UCAL/MPS/DLR/IDA/NASA; 13 top left Mercury: Johns Hopkins University/APL/NASA; 14 bottom thermometer: digitalgenetics/iStockphoto; 14-15 all other images: NASA; 16 center left bird: Benny Rytter/iStockphoto; 16 top center rocket: NASA; 16 bottom right lion: Eric Isselee/iStockphoto; 16-17 Earth background: USGS/NASA; 17 top left butterflies: thawats/iStockphoto; 17 center right Earth: Karsten Schneider/Science Source; 18-19 all other images: NASA; 19 top left Earth: USGS/NASA; 20 center: NASA; 20 top left, 20 top right and throughout: clusterx/Fotolia; 20-21 background and throughout: ESO/Serge Brunier, Frederic Tapissier/NASA; 22 bottom center: yganko/iStockphoto; 22 bottom right: yganko/iStockphoto; 22 bottom left: Kgkarolina/iStockphoto; 23 top sky: Son Gallery - Wilson Lee/Getty Images; 23 bottom right: yganko/iStockphoto; 23 bottom center: AlexanderZam/iStockphoto; 23 bottom left: rendixalextian/

iStockphoto; 24-25 Mars: Stocktrek Images/Getty Images; 25 center right moon: JPL-Caltech/University of Arizona/NASA; 25 center left moon: G. Neukum (FU Berlin), Mars Express, DLR, ESA/NASA; 26 center: JPL-Caltech/MSSS/NASA; 28-29 main: Joel Kowsky/NASA; 30 top left flies: Antagain/iStockphoto; 30 center bottom right: DebbiSmirnoff/iStockphoto; 30 center bottom left: Neil Lockhart/Shutterstock, Inc.; 30 bottom left: fotofermer/iStockphoto; 30 bottom right: Antagain/iStockphoto; 30 center top right: Francois Gohier/Science Source; 30 center left top: LEGO/JPL-Caltech/KSC/NASA; 31 top center: Dmitry Lovetsky/AP Images; 31 top right: NASA; 31 bottom left: Marc Tielemans/Alamy Images; 31 bottom right soccerball: Samuray/iStockphoto; 31 center right spiders: Jeffrey Schreier/iStockphoto; 31 top left: Francois Gohier/Science Source; 32-33 all images: NASA; 34-35 main: Andrey Armyagov/Shutterstock, Inc.; 36-37 all images: NASA; 38 all images: NASA; 40 all other asteroids: Science Photo Library/Alamy Images; 40 Kleopatra asteroid: JPL/NASA; 41 bottom background: NASA; 41 asteroids: Science Photo Library/Alamy Images; 42 top right: NASA; 42 bottom right: ESA/AOES/NASA; 42-43 background: NASA; 43 top Jupiter: ESA/Amy Simon (Goddard Space Flight Center)/NASA; 44 center left: JPL-Caltech/NASA; 44 all other images: NASA; 44-45 top background: JPL/Space Science Institute/NASA; 45 all other images: NASA; 46 Uranus: Lawrence

Sromovsky, (Univ. Wisconsin-Madison), Keck Observatory/NASA; 47 Neptune: JPL/NASA; 47 center right: JPL-Caltech/NASA; 48 top right Sun: SDO/NASA; 48-49 Voyager space probe: NASA; 49 top center planet: ESA/Amy Simon (Goddard Space Flight Center)/NASA; 49 top right planet: JPL/Space Science Institute/NASA; 50-51 background: Johns Hopkins University Applied Physics Laboratory/Southwest Research Institute/NASA; 52 center: ESA/AOES Medialab/NASA; 54 bottom background: Thomas Tuchan/iStockphoto; 54 center Kepler space telescope: NASA; 55 center right planets: The Planetary Habitability Laboratory @ UPR Arecibo, Discovery: Robert A. Wittenmyer (UNSW Australia)/NASA; 56-57 background: NASA; 56-57 planets: PHL @ UPR Arecibo (phl.upr.edu), ESA/Hubble/NASA; 58 center left: Debra Meloy Elmegreen (Vassar College) & the Hubble Heritage Team (AURA/STScI)/NASA; 58-59 Hubble Space Telescope: NASA; 59 top background: NASA; 59 magnifying glass: kyoshino/iStockphoto; 59 bottom right: Eraxion/iStockphoto; 60 center left: Victor Habbick Visions/Science Source; 60 center right: AstroStar/Shutterstock, Inc.; 60 bottom right: Science Photo Library/Alamy Images; 60-61 stars background: AstroStar/Shutterstock, Inc.; 60-61 moon background: Goddard/Lunar Reconnaissance Orbiter/NASA; 62-63 bottom background: Dr. Timothy Parker, JPL/NASA; 63 right top left: Volodymyr Kyrylyuk/iStockphoto; 63 right top

right: Bulgac/iStockphoto; 63 right center left: urbancow/iStockphoto; 63 right center right: andresr/iStockphoto; 63 right bottom left: &#169 Editorial12/iStockphoto; 63 right bottom right: caracterdesign/iStockphoto; 64 top left: Ames/JPL-Caltech/NASA.

All LEGO® illustrations by Paul Lee.

> That was far out! Let's go home to Earth.